D0493442

Claude Monet
Paintings of the Seine and the Sea

FRANCES FOWLE

NATIONAL GALLERIES
OF SCOTLAND

Introduction

1 *Entrance to Vétheuil, Winter*, 1879
Göteborg Museum of Art, Sweden

Claude Monet 1840–1926 is best known as the painter of water lilies and poppy fields, rather than of rivers and sea cliffs. However, the most prolific period of his career, from the autumn of 1878 to the spring of 1883, was spent painting on the river Seine at Vétheuil and working on the Normandy coast. During this short time, Monet produced no fewer than 300 pictures, his impressive output motivated to a great extent by his rising debts and, initially, by anxiety concerning his wife's health. Many of the landscapes that he painted at Vétheuil were rural idylls designed to appeal to a bourgeois, urban public: weekenders and holiday-makers seeking an escape from the noise and bustle of the city. However, this was also one of the most significant periods in Monet's development as an artist, and the strikingly novel images that he produced on the Normandy coast move beyond Impressionism, foreshadowing the early 'series' paintings which he was to execute during his years at Giverny.

Monet and the Hoschedé Family

In 1874 Monet's *Impression, Sunrise* was shown at the first exhibition of a group of independent artists in the studio of the photographer, Nadar. The sketchy handling of the paintings exhibited outraged the public. Of Monet's work, one critic wrote that it had been 'executed by the infantile hand of a school child who is spreading out colours on any sort of surface for the first time': another wrote that 'wallpaper in its embryonic state is more finished than that seascape'.

Nevertheless, Monet's picture gave a name to an entire new movement in art: Impressionism. It also found a buyer. This was Ernest Hoschedé (1837–1891), a Parisian businessman, who inherited a fortune, both from his father's business (he was a merchant of fine laces and

2 *The Artist's Garden at Vétheuil*, 1881
National Gallery of Art, Washington. Ailsa Mellon Bruce Collection.

shawls), and from his marriage in 1863 to Alice Raingo, who came from a wealthy Belgian family. Alice and Ernest divided their time between their luxurious Paris apartment at 64 Rue de Lisbonne and the Château de Rottembourg at Montgeron where they entertained on a lavish scale, even chartering a special train to transport guests from the city. Hoschedé inherited a love of art from his uncle, who left him his entire collection of French nineteenth-century paintings. Ernest went on to develop a passion for the work of the Impressionists, especially Monet and Sisley, and he became one of the most important early patrons of Impressionist art. By 1877 he owned sixteen works by Monet, as well as pictures by Sisley, Pissarro and Renoir. He commissioned Monet to paint four large decorative panels in his house at Montgeron, which the artist completed between 1876 and 1877. During this period Monet and the Hoschedés became close friends and when Ernest's extravagant lifestyle eventually caught up with him and he was financially ruined, Monet was swift to offer his support. Hoschedé's large collection of Impressionist paintings was sold in June 1878. The pictures went for disappointingly low prices and Ernest fled to Belgium to escape his debts. The Hoschedés were forced to abandon their life of luxury and in August 1878, at Monet's suggestion, they moved into a small house in the village of Vétheuil, together with the artist, his wife, Camille, and their two children, Jean and Michel.

Vétheuil

3 *The Church at Vétheuil*, 1878
National Gallery of Scotland, Edinburgh

Vétheuil is a picturesque, unspoiled village, situated on the right bank of the river Seine, about sixty kilometres north of Paris. In Monet's day, unlike Argenteuil, where the artist had previously been living, it was neither a favourite spot for holidaymakers – since it offered little in the way of leisure pursuits – nor easy for commuters, since the only link with the capital was by railway from Mantes, a twelve kilometre carriage ride away. Most of the small population of 622 residents made their living from the land.

Monet took a house on the Route de Mantes but, with the Hoschedés and their six children, they numbered twelve in total, as well as a handful of servants, and they were soon forced to move to a larger house, situated on the road from Vétheuil to La Roche-Guyon. It was owned by a Mme Eve Elliot who lived nearby at Les Tourelles, an imposing mansion, whose distinctive turrets feature in several of Monet's views of the village, including the enchanting snow scene *Entrance to Vétheuil, Winter*, 1879 [plate 1]. Monet's house had a large garden, leading down to the river where he tethered his studio boat. In 1881 he painted the garden in full bloom and bathed in shimmering light. *The Artist's Garden at Véthueil* [plate 2] includes three figures – probably one of the Hoschedé daughters standing on the steps with Monet's younger son, Michel, and four-year-old Jean-Pierre Hoschedé in the foreground. Absent from the scene is the Monets' elder son, Jean, who was born in Paris in August 1867. Monet married Jean's mother, Camille Doncieux, three years later in June 1870. Their second child, Michel, was born on 17 March 1878, only a few months before the move to Vétheuil. From the moment the baby was born, Camille's health, which had been bad for some time, began to deteriorate, marking the beginning of a period of constant anxiety for Monet.

4 *Vétheuil in Summer*, 1880
The Metropolitan Museum of Art, New York. Bequest of William Church Osborn, 1951

Soon after the two families had settled in Vétheuil, Ernest Hoschedé gained a position with the Paris newspaper *Le Voltaire*. This meant he spent most of his time in the capital, leaving Alice and the family in Vétheuil where the rent was cheaper. Meanwhile, Monet was having difficulty selling his paintings and, to make matters worse, Camille was in need of almost constant care. Any money that Monet made from selling his pictures, when it was not spent on paints and materials, went towards buying medicine. As their financial situation worsened, Monet fell behind with the rent and was unable to pay the servants' wages. It was not long before the children's nanny and tutor both handed in their notice.

Looking at the pictures that Monet produced during this period in Vétheuil there is little evidence of the difficulties he was undergoing in his private life. Although his letters are full of self-pity and pleas for financial assistance, his paintings, by contrast, are bursting with sunshine, colour and luminosity. One of the earliest paintings that he completed at Vétheuil was *The Church at Vétheuil* [plate 3], a view of the church of Notre Dame with its splendid sixteenth-century façade. The church was not only the religious and social centre of the village but also the dominating feature of Monet's views of Vétheuil. He painted it in different seasons from the opposite bank of the river or from his studio boat. In *Vétheuil in Summer* [plate 4], the church is depicted in loose brushstrokes, its silhouette reflected in the tranquil waters of the Seine. A slender poplar on the river bank draws the eye towards the tall steeple in the centre of the painting. This is a summer scene, but on several occasions Monet painted the same view covered in a blanket of snow. In *Vétheuil in Winter* of 1879 [plate 5] he uses cool blues, greys and violets to convey the bitter cold of a winter's day. Despite the ice floes on the river the ferry still appears to be operating, carrying passengers to

5 *Vétheuil in Winter*, 1879
Frick Collection, New York

6 *Lavacourt, Sun and Snow*, 1879
National Gallery, London

Lavacourt on the opposite bank where Monet had set up his easel.

The notion of painting the same view at different seasons of the year was also practised by Monet's fellow Impressionist, Sisley, in his paintings at Louveciennes. Monet developed this practice, not only in his views of Vétheuil, but in his images of the nearby village of Lavacourt, a collection of houses huddled together along the banks of the river Seine. In 1879, Monet painted the village in snow – as in *Lavacourt, Sun and Snow* [plate 6], picking out the sunlit, distant hills with bold flecks of pink and lilac – and also in sunshine. Sometimes he painted the scene from the Vétheuil side as in *Lavacourt* of 1880 [plate 7], taking in the broad sweep of the river and the vast expanse of intensely blue sky.

In the spring of 1879 Monet took part in the Fourth Impressionist Exhibition which was held in a new building at 28 avenue de l'Opéra in

7 *Lavacourt*, 1880
Dallas Museum of Art. Munger Fund

8 *Camille Monet on her Deathbed*, 1879
Musée d'Orsay, Paris

Paris. He sent twenty-nine paintings, which were hung in the final room, alongside the work of Pissarro. He did not attend the exhibition, as Camille was extremely ill and almost certainly dying. By August 1879 she was unable to get out of bed or hold down any food and Monet's entire time was taken up with looking after her. On 31 August a priest was called to the house to administer the last rites and to sanction her marriage to Monet (which had been conducted in a civil ceremony in 1870). Five days later she died at the age of thirty-two. Monet was devastated. He painted her on her deathbed, shrouded in a veil of white and blue brushstrokes – *Camille Monet on her Deathbed* [plate 8] – in a last desperate attempt to preserve her memory.

After Camille's death rumours began to spread about Monet's relationship with Alice Hoschedé. Ernest was unwilling to give up his job in Paris and Alice was reluctant to join him there. That year Hoschedé did not even return to his family for Christmas. In January 1880 *Le Gaulois* newspaper announced a mock funeral, reporting the 'grievous loss' of Claude Monet who was living in Vétheuil with his 'charming wife' (Alice Hoschedé). The article went on to report that Monet supported his former patron, Ernest Hoschedé, who was financially bankrupt and living in the artist's studio in Paris.

In truth, Monet was hardly able to support himself. He was now six months behind with the rent and was relying more and more on his friend, the artist Gustave Caillebotte, to lend him money. That Christmas the Monet children received no presents from their father and he spent much of the winter of 1879–80 painting still lifes in the hope that they would sell more easily than his landscapes. But his debts continued to mount and in February 1880 the servants, tired of working for no pay, handed in their notice. The bleakness of Monet's own life was reflected in one of the harshest winters on record. The thermometer fell so low

9 *The Break up of the Ice*, 1880
The University of Michigan Museum of Art, Ann Arbor, Michigan. Acquired through the generosity of Russell B. Stearns (LS&A 1916) and his wife Andrée B. Stearns, Dedham, Massachusetts, 1976/2.134

that the river Seine froze over. Once the thaw set in huge blocks of ice began to force their way down river, crashing into each other with such force that Monet and his family were woken from their sleep. Monet worked through the winter to capture this beautiful and eerie spectacle in a group of about a dozen stark and abstract canvases such as *The Break up of the Ice* [plate 9], some of which appear to prefigure his later water lily paintings.

In June 1880 Monet exhibited a number of his 'floating ice' paintings at his first solo exhibition at the gallery of *La Vie Moderne*, a weekly publication run by Georges Charpentier, the publisher of Emile Zola's novels and an important early patron of the Impressionists. In the exhibition catalogue Théodore Duret described how the artist, 'despite the season ... leaves his studio and works outdoors under the open sky'. Monet had set up his easel in subzero conditions to execute these paintings and he liked to encourage the myth that they were completed entirely in the open air. We now know that Monet's dedication to painting outside was not as rigorous as he liked to indicate and that, although he would spend several sittings working in front of the subject, many of his pictures were improved in the studio at a later stage.

The previous month Monet had been described in the press by Zola as the 'leading Impressionist', and many of the pictures in the exhibition sold almost immediately. In particular, Mme Charpentier acquired the stunning *Floating Ice* (now in the Shelburne Museum of Art, Vermont) as a present for her husband. It seemed that things were looking up at last. Monet was beginning to achieve modest success and recognition, and it would not be long before he was able to repay his debts.

Painting on the Normandy coast

10 *The Sea at Fécamp*, 1881
Staatsgalerie, Stuttgart

In the autumn of 1880 Monet spent a short holiday with his brother Léon on the Normandy coast. This brief sojourn marked the beginning of a four-year campaign, focusing on the soaring cliffs and dramatic coastline at Fécamp, Pourville and Etretat. Monet's work of this period began to develop in an entirely new direction, a far cry from his suburban landscapes of the 1870s. His work of this period is characterised by unusual viewpoints and decorative tendencies, many of his pictures are veiled in an atmospheric haze, and in general he moves towards a more abstract approach to painting. The first signs of this new direction in Monet's work are in the pictures he produced in the fishing port of Fécamp, where he was staying in the spring of 1880. Paintings such as *The Sea at Fécamp* [plate 10] of 1881 have an invigorating quality, and a wildness and freedom of handling quite absent in his earlier work. Significantly, these stylistic tendencies coincide with the renewed support of his Paris dealer Durand-Ruel, giving him freedom at last from financial worries.

In October 1881 the lease on Monet's house at Vétheuil came to an end. Monet and Alice moved into a small house behind the post office for a couple of months before relocating to Poissy, also situated on the river Seine, but closer to Paris. One of the main reasons for choosing Poissy was that it provided better schooling for the children, but it had the added benefit of offering the whole family a fresh start after the death of Camille and the separation of Alice and Ernest Hoschedé. Here Monet rented a large house, the villa Saint-Louis, with a view of the river. Stationed at an upstairs window he painted an unusual view of anglers fishing from their boats in *Fisherman at Poissy* 1882 (now in the Osterreichische Galerie Belvedere, Vienna), one of only four pictures that he completed in Poissy itself.

By comparison with tranquil and picturesque Vétheuil, Monet found

11 *Fishing Nets at Pourville*, 1882
Gemeentemuseum, The Hague

12 *The Church at Varengeville*, 1882
Barber Institute of Fine Arts, The University of Birmingham

the town 'horrible'. He packed his bags and painting materials and set off for the coastal town of Dieppe, booking into a room in the Grand Hotel du Nord et Victoria. Finding the landscape of Dieppe too urban he swiftly moved along the coast to Pourville, a tiny fishing village, where Alice and the extended family joined him for the summer months. He stayed initially in a hotel/restaurant called *A la Renommée des Galettes*, run by Paul and Eugénie Graff, known affectionately as Le Père and La Mère Paul. Monet captured the couple on canvas in two lively and engaging portraits, which he offered to them as a gift.

At Pourville Monet discovered a variety of suitable subjects, ranging from spectacular cliff walks to fishing nets drying on the beach, as in *Fishing Nets at Pourville* [plate 11]. Among the most atmospheric pictures of this period are his views of the church at Varengeville, perched dramatically above the sea cliff and the Gorge des Moutiers in *The Church at Varengeville* [plate 12]. He soon became attached to one particular subject close to Pourville, an abandoned Napoleonic customs officer's cottage overlooking the English Channel at Varengeville, as seen in *Rising Tide at Pourville* [plate 13], and to which he returned time and again, completing fourteen different canvases during the course of the summer.

We know from Monet's letters that most of these studies were painted over ten or so sessions, and that some took as many as twenty sittings. On any given day he worked on up to eight different canvases, changing each canvas as the atmospheric conditions altered. This was the first group of paintings in Monet's career that amounted to what could be described as a 'series' and in this they prefigure the better-known images of the 1890s – the haystacks, poplars and Rouen cathedral. These works took the Impressionist aesthetic to its natural conclusion. Instead of capturing a particular moment on canvas – a passing effect of light or weather – Monet captured several such

13 *Rising Tide at Pourville*, 1882
Brooklyn Museum of Art, New York. Gift of Mrs Horace Havemeyer 41.1260

14 *Sunset, Etretat*, 1883
Musée des Beaux-Arts de Nancy

moments, so that, when viewed together, the paintings give the impression of time passing.

Monet included thirty-five works in the Seventh Impressionist Exhibition of 1882. By this date his paintings were fetching reasonable prices. Yet fellow artists such as Sisley and Pissarro were still finding it difficult to sell their work and the public at large remained uncomfortable with the sketchiness and inconsequential subject matter of Impressionist painting. Some critics even suggested that the pervasive blue-violet tonality typical of Impressionism was symptomatic of some kind of visual disorder suffered by the artists.

The following year, in January 1883, Monet moved along the Normandy coast to Etretat, booking into a room at the Hotel Blanquet, overlooking the sea. This rocky coast had attracted many artists before Monet, including Boudin, Corot, Daubigny, Jongkind and especially Courbet. Monet was clearly inspired by Courbet's paintings of landmarks such as the Aiguille and the Porte d'Aval – the rocky promontory with its flying buttress-like formation which sticks out into the sea – and he had already visited and painted at Etretat in 1868–9. Works such as *Sunset, Etretat* of 1883 [plate 14] recall the atmospheric works of the Dutch artist Jongkind. In *Rough Sea, Etretat* [plate 15] Monet transforms Courbet's tranquil vision of the Porte d'Aval into his own, more turbulent and exciting image.

Not content to paint the subjects on his doorstep, Monet ventured farther afield, gaining access to the Manneporte, a huge mass of rock, hollowed out over the centuries by the constant battering of wind and sea, and accessible only by clambering through a hole in the cliff wall at low tide. In *The Manneporte, Etretat* [plate 16] he focuses on the sublime and monumental form of the rock as it plunges into the boiling and frothing sea. Only the tiny figures standing beneath the dramatic arch

give a sense of the vastness of this extraordinary geological feature. The surface of the painting is divided into elemental water, sky and rock. The brushstrokes shimmer and glitter, creating a new luminosity and intensity of expression.

15 *Rough Sea, Etretat, 1883*
Musée des Beaux Arts de Lyon

Postscript

In April 1883 Monet and Alice moved to Giverny, a small farming village situated between Paris and Rouen. They rented a pink stucco house called *Le Pressoir* or 'The Cider Press' with two-and-a-half acres of land, later transformed by Monet into the beautiful gardens and lily ponds which can be visited today. Monet bought the house in 1890 and two years later, after the death of the unfortunate Ernest Hoschedé, married Alice in a civil ceremony.

Monet's fortunes had taken a decided upturn and he was beginning to make a name for himself as an artist. A major retrospective of his work at the Galerie Georges Petit in 1889 boosted sales of his work and the exhibitions of his paintings of haystacks and poplars at Durand-Ruel's in 1891 and 1892 enjoyed a runaway success. The worries and anxieties of his years at Vétheuil seemed a distant memory. And yet the notion of painting a series of images developed from the work that he produced on the Seine and on the Normandy coast. The paintings of Vétheuil and Lavacourt in summer and winter prefigure the haystacks and poplars, painted at different seasons of the year. The sublime image of the Manneporte foreshadows the towering façade of Rouen Cathedral. And the abstract paintings of breaking ice on the Seine at Vétheuil and of breaking waves on the sea at Fécamp paved the way for the famous water lily paintings for which Monet is chiefly remembered today.

16 *The Manneporte*, Etretat, 1883
The Metropolitan Museum of Art, New York. Bequest of William Church Osborn, 1951

Brief biography

1840 Oscar-Claude Monet born in Paris on 14 November, early years spent in Le Havre.

1856–7 Meets Boudin and, at his suggestion, works on his first landscape and outdoor paintings.

1859–61 Moves to Paris and works at the Académie Suisse where he meets Pissarro.

1861–2 Military service in Algiera. On discharge from the army due to ill health, he returns to Paris and enters Gleyre's studio where he meets Bazille, Renoir and Sisley.

1863 Works in the forest of Fontainebleau with Bazille.

1866 Success at the Salon with *Camille in a Green Dress*, a portrait of his future wife Camille Doncieux.

1867 Birth of his son, Jean.

1870 Marries Camille in a civil ceremony. They move to London where Monet studies the work of Constable and Turner and becomes acquainted with the art dealer, Durand-Ruel.

1872 Settles at Argenteuil and is joined there by Sisley.

1873 Forms a friendship with the artist, Gustave Caillebotte.

1874 Takes part in the first of the eight Impressionist exhibitions.

1876 Start of the friendship between the Monet and Hoschedé families.

1877 Spends September at Montgeron. Ernest Hoschedé financially ruined.

1878 The Hoschedés' properties sold at auction. Alice Hoschedé and her six children move to Vétheuil with the Monet family. Birth of Monet's second son, Michel.

1879 Camille Monet dies. Alice looks after the eight children.

1881 Makes a trip to the Normandy coast and a painting expedition to Dieppe. Monet, Alice and the children move to Poissy.

1882 Makes trips to Pourville and the surrounding area.

1883 Painting expeditions to Le Havre and Etretat and travels with Renoir to the Mediterranean. In March has a one-man show at Durand-Ruel's. Moves to Giverny.

1885 Exhibits at the Exposition Internationale at George Petit's galleries.

1886 Paints in Holland. Shows with the Groupe des Vingt in Brussels.

1890 Buys house in Giverny. Works on his series paintings of haystacks.

1891 Ernest Hoschedé dies. Monet visits London.

1892 Monet marries Alice Hoschedé.

[illegible] Begins the creation of his famo[illegible] ga[illegible]en with lily ponds at Giverny.

1895 Paints in Norway. Paints a series based on the water lilies in the pond at Giverny.

1897 Blanche Hoschedé marries Monet's son, Jean. *Rouen Cathedral* series exhibited in Venice at the Biennale.

1899–1901 Visits London several times to see his son, Michel, who is at school there and works on the *Thames* series

1904 Visits the Prado in Spain to see the work of Velázquez.

1908 Last painting trip to Venice. Monet's eyesight begins to fail.

1911 Alice Monet dies in May.

1914 Monet's son, Jean, dies.

1921 Monet's sight deteriorates further and he has difficulty working.

1923 Undergoes a cataract operation on his right eye and starts work again at the end of the year.

1926 Monet dies on 5 December.

Published by the Trustees of
the National Galleries of Scotland
on the occasion of the exhibition
Monet: the Seine and the Sea held
at the Royal Scottish Academy,
Edinburgh from 2 August
to 26 October 2003

ISBN 1 903278 45 7

Cover: *Lavacourt*, 1880
Dallas Museum of Art, Munger Fund

Pages one and two: *Sunset, Etretat*, 1883
North Carolina Museum of Art, Raleigh

Designed and typeset by Dalrymple
Printed in China by Toppan Printing
Company (Shenzhen Limited)

The exhibition, *Monet: the Seine
and the Sea*, is sponsored by

If you have enjoyed this book
and would like more information,
the catalogue which accompanies
the exhibition is available from:

Publications Department
National Galleries of Scotland
Belford Rd · Edinburgh EH4 3DS